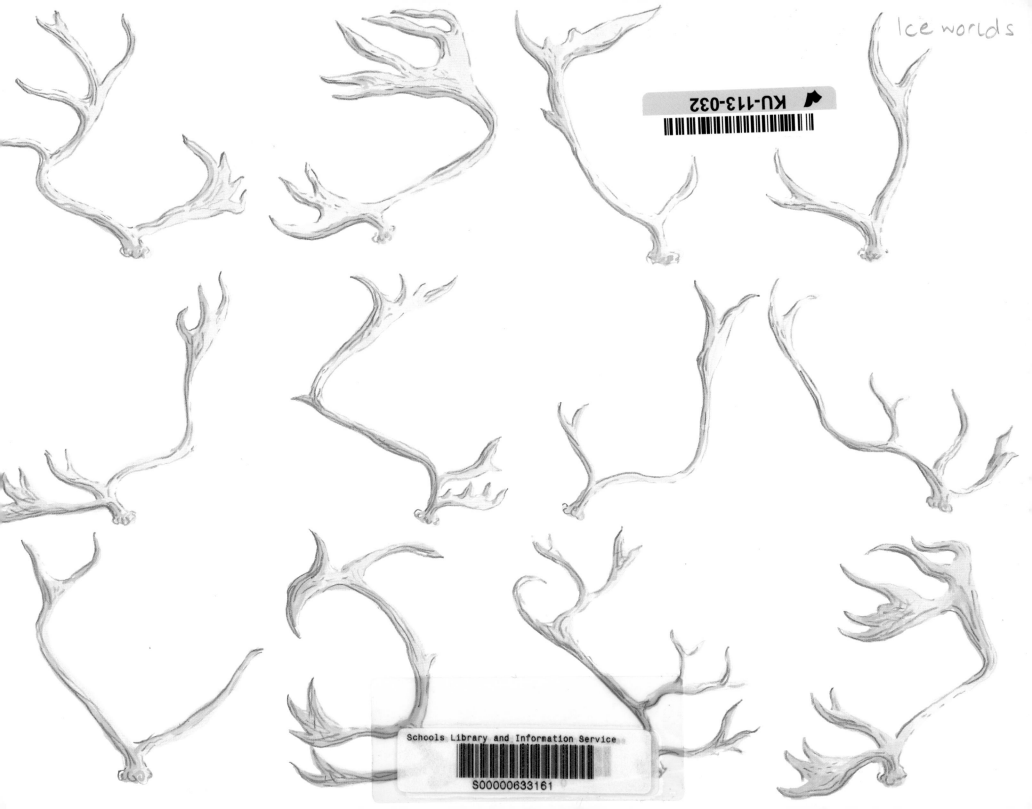

Ice worlds

IF YOU TRAVEL NORTH from anywhere in the world, eventually you will reach a land of snow and ice. Just before the permanent snowline is the tundra – vast flat plains with no trees and little vegetation other than lichens and grasses. These barren lands are the calving grounds for many herds of caribou; they travel here for the brief summer through harsh winds and driving snow. Caribou and reindeer are the deer of the North; this book tells the story of one of the groups of caribou that make up the Bathurst herd.

CARIBOU JOURNEY

Vivian French

Illustrated by Lisa Flather

THE INUIT PEOPLE call it the Wandering Time...
It begins early in February. A group of caribou are feeding
near a lake in the Northern Territories. Both land and
frozen lake are thickly covered in snow. The snow is
at least fifty five centimetres deep, and even though
it is nearly midday and the sun is shining, the temperature
is minus thirty degrees centigrade.

A female, one of her ears ragged from some accident
or wolf attack, lowers her head to sniff the snow.
After a moment or two she paws at it, digging
a hole with a front hoof. She clears a patch of
ground and begins to feed on the lichen and other tiny
plants. A male wanders up beside her, but she turns her
antlered head towards him and he walks away. Her need for
food is greater than his – she will give birth in the summer.
Her last year's calf, now eight months old, moves closer,
and Ragged Ear shifts a little so that Soft Ear can feed too.

DARKNESS COMES EARLY, but Ragged Ear and Soft Ear are still feeding. The lichen is sparse here; it does not take long to clear the patches that they find. They and the other caribou sniff the snow, or plunge their noses deep down into the dry white powdery chill to check for the scent of food beneath. If they find the scent, they dig, feed... and move on.

Only the raven flying home to roost can see that there is a direction in the way that Ragged Ear is moving. Almost imperceptibly she is moving north, Soft Ear following closely behind her.

THROUGHOUT MARCH Ragged Ear and her daughter
continue to wander steadily northwards, sometimes one
kilometre a day, sometimes two. The weather is not good.
There are terrible storms lasting for days at a time with
howling winds of more than eighty kilometres per hour.
The snow swirls day and night, but caribou have thick
long-haired coats and Ragged Ear has seen winters worse
than this. From time to time she turns her back
to the strongest of the winds as she continues her endless
search for food. Soft Ear shakes her head as flurries of snow
whip seven metres up into the air above her; it is difficult
to tell where the clouds end and the snow begins.

Other females and their calves are nearby. They too are
taking the first steps on the long journey to the calving
grounds. The males have been left behind, many of them
sheltering among the twisted and stunted trees thirty
kilometres to the south.

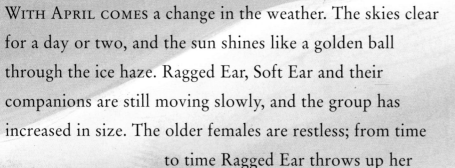

With April comes a change in the weather. The skies clear for a day or two, and the sun shines like a golden ball through the ice haze. Ragged Ear, Soft Ear and their companions are still moving slowly, and the group has increased in size. The older females are restless; from time to time Ragged Ear throws up her head as if she is listening for some soundless call.

Soft Ear watches a little anxiously; the regular pattern of the last few months is changing, and she is not sure what to expect.

The snow is different now. The soft dry powder that the caribou could easily dig away, has crusted, and is harder and heavier. So, although the days stay lighter for longer, it is more difficult to find food.

It has begun.

The silent message has come, and been understood.
Ragged Ear stands still for a moment, and then begins
walking, slowly, steadily, resolutely – always heading north.
Soft Ear is behind her, treading in her mother's footsteps.
A few metres further back plods another female and her
calf, then another, and another. They walk in single file,
one behind the other, until the line is nearly
four hundred caribou long.

A ridge is directly in front of them. They do not pause, but head up the snow-covered rocks. Their round broad hooves tread safely over the rough ground. By the time the last animals pass, the snow is beaten solid into a gleaming ribbon of white ice.

THE WOLVES SPRING with a snarling growling snapping of teeth. Ragged Ear leaps away in a cloud of flying snow, Soft Ear bounding close beside her. Other caribou follow – speed is their protection, but the rocks slow them down. The wolves have chosen their ambush point well.

A young wolf marks down the smallest of the calves as he runs this way and that. The struggle ends cleanly and swiftly and a gush of scarlet stains the snow.

Ragged Ear, panting, reaches the top of the ridge and stops. The calf inside her stirs, and she feels again the urgent call to reach the summer grazing. She looks nervously over her shoulder, and then begins to walk... on and on. Soft Ear takes her place behind her mother, and once more a line of caribou stretches out against the evening skyline.

THE RAVEN, flying high in the crisp late April morning, sees more and more and yet more lines of caribou crossing the frozen barren lands beneath him. The lines meet, interweave and mingle with each other, and the single threads become a moving cloak, rippling across the whiteness of the snow. The raven sees the steam of the animals' breath hanging like a cloud above them.

Ragged Ear and Soft Ear are moving more slowly now. The last few days were easy, travelling on the flat, ice-covered surface of Contwoyto Lake, but now the trail leads up and along a rocky valley. The sun is warm enough to soften the snow in the middle of the day, and walking through it is hard. Often the herds have to stop and wait until the afternoon chill crusts the snow once more.

THE THAW CONTINUES. It is early May, and there is a river to cross. The Mara is in full flood, with ice floes crashing and roaring as they smash and grind against each other. An older female plods along the river bank, beside the roaring torrent. Ragged Ear and the others follow behind.

About three kilometres higher up the river is wider. The water is a whirling slush of churning ice and mud, but this time there is no hesitation. The old caribou plunges in, neck deep, and swims steadily across. Ragged Ear and Soft Ear wait for a fraction of a second, then they too wade in. Behind them tens, twenties, fifties, hundreds and yet more hundreds of caribou follow on.

On the far bank, the wolves are waiting.

THEY ARE CUNNING, the wolves. Ragged Ear is heavily weighed down with her unborn calf, but she is big and strong, and her antlers ride proudly on her head as she heaves her dripping body out of the water. Soft Ear is tucked safely behind her. The wolves watch and let them pass. But an old caribou stumbles...

This time the killing takes longer. The old caribou fights to the last, and at least one of the wolves is sent flying through the air, as she kicks and bellows and struggles for her life.

Other caribou charge each other and buck and rear in panic. Some try to escape into the river, but they are driven back by the relentless oncoming waves of heads and horns. At last the old caribou shudders and dies – no more now than a heap of torn flesh. The wolf pack closes in to feed.

Ragged Ear is once again walking steadily north. But where is Soft Ear?

SOFT EAR IS RUNNING. Up and down the long winding column she runs, calling for her mother. She thinks she sees Ragged Ear, but she is wrong. The stranger has no time for another calf, her own yearling is trotting behind her. Soft Ear calls again, runs again. Up and down, up and down, up and down, until at last she tires. Wearily she follows the last of the line.

Has Ragged Ear noticed that her daughter is missing?
It is difficult to say. She is striding ever onwards, her mind set on reaching the birthing grounds.

MAY HAS GONE, and with the coming of
June much of the snow has melted.
The sky is overcast and the air is damp
and foggy, but the herds of female caribou are
moving still. Ragged Ear holds her head
high. The air smells different. There is,
perhaps, a tang of salt. She is so
nearly there – the wide sweep
of the birthing grounds
are spread out before her.

One last effort and she is at the end of her journey.
She collapses. All around her other females are doing
the same. More and more and more caribou follow.
More and more sink down exhausted.

One small yearling calf is the last to stagger over
the tussocky ground and sink to her knees –
Soft Ear has made her first journey.

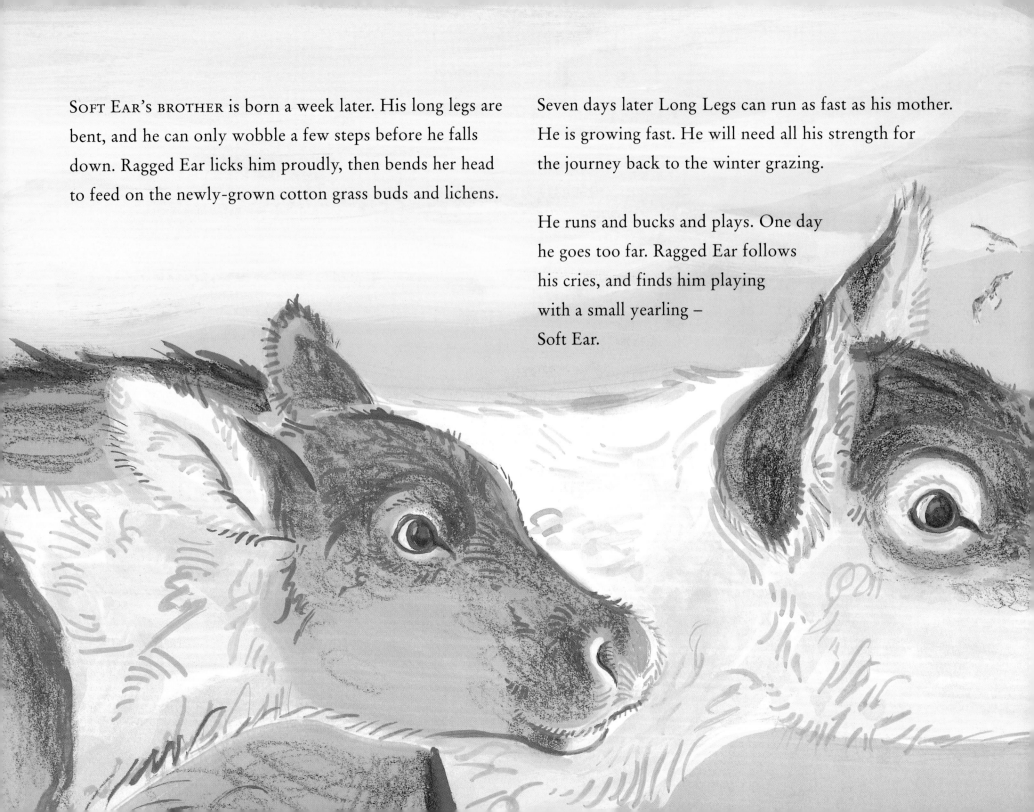

SOFT EAR'S BROTHER is born a week later. His long legs are bent, and he can only wobble a few steps before he falls down. Ragged Ear licks him proudly, then bends her head to feed on the newly-grown cotton grass buds and lichens.

Seven days later Long Legs can run as fast as his mother. He is growing fast. He will need all his strength for the journey back to the winter grazing.

He runs and bucks and plays. One day he goes too far. Ragged Ear follows his cries, and finds him playing with a small yearling – Soft Ear.

For Nap, with much love, V.F.
To Jayne and Sarah, L.F.

First published in Great Britain in 2001 by Zero To Ten Limited
327 High Street, Slough, Berkshire, SL1 1TX

Publisher: Anna McQuinn
Art Director: Tim Foster
Senior Editor: Simona Sideri
Publishing Assistant: Vikram Parashar

A CIP catalogue record for this book is available from the British Library.

ISBN 1-84089-197-1

Printed in Hong Kong